Love :: In Code

Love :: In Code

❧

Spiritual Steps

to

Addiction Recovery

Barbara Permilla Roth

ISBN: 978-0-9906003-3-6
ISBN: 0990600335
Library of Congress Control Number: 2014913051
Paradise & Co., West Lake Hills, Texas

Dedication

To You

The Code
The [Code] is Love.
To be in Code is to Love.
Addictions are Spiritual injuries.
In essence, our souls go out of Code.
Our souls renew to Love and return to Code.

Contents

Preface

To recover is love Discovered.

Breathe in the royal midnight blue of Jerusalem, for peace is present. Daylight beckons.

So much has been written about addictions. Yet how much closer do we honestly think we are to arresting addictions forever, or even preventing them in the first place?

Knowledge can't completely help against addictions. Intelligent people can become addicts. They know better.

It seems each day brings forth a new substance ready to attack us. To be controlled by an addiction is a condition full of shame for the individual, and heartache for their loved ones.

Love :: In Code is the account of the spiritual journey I traveled away from addiction toward an enduring recovery. It was to a destiny I truly thought I would never reach.

On this passage I began navigating Kabbalah texts, and experienced an awakening. It is from God's in code connection that we are created out of love to love.

Kabbalah reveals the Creator to mankind. It is a set of teachings that studies the system— *the sequence and force that governs nature*—the code of our world. Kabbalah is not about obtaining belief in Divinity, but about the revelation of it.

The word *Kabbalah* is derived from the Hebrew verb *lekabel*, meaning "to receive." It is not a religion and it is open for all to study its wisdom. Still, Kabbalah is integrated with Judaism—in that it unveils the Torah, a spiritual collection of the first five books of the Hebrew Bible.

With compass and guidebook in hand, the presence of stars gathered me to the home of closeness I had longed for. My prayer is that some thought or word herein may influence a step toward your own healing, to your own belonging.

For you see, my dear *Love :: In Code* readers, there is always hope where there is Love. Of this I write.

Barbara Permilla Roth

Step 1

The Turn

Love is a revolution in your Heart.

The number of times I either quit smoking cigarettes or struggled to stop smoking are innumerable, totally innumerable. I was highly resistant to treatments. I had reached the point that should the mere thought of quitting yet again enter my mind, I knew better than to mention it to anyone. Friends and family were skeptical in their vision of my success. Well, for that matter, so was I.

There are many smokers—millions—who one day simply decide they no longer wish to smoke. It is easy for them. I am not in that group, and that is not my story.

There are also millions of people who struggle with numerous attempts to quit smoking, and then one day through determination, they succeed. Although it may appear I am in that group, I am not, and that is not my story.

I had used up all attempts at any recovery. I had no strength to quit smoking, and I had resigned myself to my nicotine addiction.

In my mind, I was a smoker and I did what smokers did. We smoked. This was the group I was in, and these were my people.

Then one day while I was hanging out, smoking, and minding my own business, I unexpectedly escaped from behind enemy lines—the addiction, and I lived to tell about it. Now, this is my story.

∽

I started smoking young. And ended up addicted.

I was an adolescent during the era when smoking was still allowed in movie theaters. Little ashtrays were embedded in the arm-rests. As the smoke bound with the projector light and streamed to the screen, it became an entrancement to me. Then, as when two lovers meet, this destined light met with the smoking and kissing on-screen. The film sets were elegant; the movie stars were intense. I was intoxicated.

Actors appeared larger than life on the widescreen, with a glamorous ambience. They exuded independence with a simmering sexual undertone. All the while they dangled a cigarette in their conversations. My mind made an association, a connection, between sexuality and smoking just as my adult identity was being formed.

Further, my mind related this independence as the characters possessing sovereignty over their lives, at the same time my teenage life felt stifled under my parents' watchful eyes. This is heady stuff. I willingly stepped into their cinematic world. It was an addiction's dream scenario—to gain control of its victim and simultaneously appear sophisticated.

Virtually everyone reached for a cigarette back then. Not everyone got addicted. I did. Addictions are devious and duplicitous like that. You get the picture.

∽◦

At the onset of this addiction, naturally, I thought I could give up smoking whenever I wanted to. Occasionally I would stop to prove I was in control. I never understood that when I would start again later, my power had been stripped from me.

Cigarette smoking may become an addiction leading to health problems. At the very, very least, the combination of tobacco residue and nicotine-filled blood may compromise your body's operating system—its code—of internal organs. If you are currently a smoker, you already know this.

There is no question that the educational material on the health dangers of smoking is absolutely needed for our precious youth. Yet I believe for some smokers that message falls on deaf ears—by the time we hear it, we're already addicted to nicotine.

So I don't want to go on about that here, because I know the power-of-knowledge component became twisted in my own mind as a scare tactic maneuver. To the last cigarette I smoked, not once did this type of persuasion help me. I read and read and read. I also smoked and smoked and smoked.

If you choose to smoke, that is your own concern. Somtimes people who have never smoked, and even former smokers, will look upon you as weak-willed if you are still smoking. They simply can't believe you would continue to light up given all the medical information about smoking.

This is all rather hurtful for smokers, as no one wants to feel shamed. Smoking at this level is a physical addiction. Smokers and nonsmokers alike should try to the best of their abilities to understand that almost everyone has some addiction, some affliction, or some vice.

Still, smoking may cause injury to your body—especially over time. If you are at present a smoker and you do want to stop, as most smokers do, but you have been having a hard go of it, please know quitting for good is possible, even for smokers who may think there is no chance. I am proof of this.

Until that time comes, whatever you do, don't think less of yourself for smoking. Don't allow anyone to act toward you in this manner, including yourself.

∽⊙

The new smoke signals are dispatching that recovery is hip. For years I aspired to be in that cool recovery clique—but I wasn't. I was never a heavy chain-smoker; nevertheless, I was a steady smoker.

Smoking was a part of my day and my life. It was a ritual I no longer wanted, but the remedy eluded me.

The happy faces of reformed smokers made it look easy to quit, though it wasn't for me. I strive to be a practical person, and I wouldn't have put myself through withdrawal so many times if I hadn't wanted to kick the habit. As a matter of record, I'd had a lot of last cigarettes before the final one.

I hated smoking; I did not want to be a smoker. Counselors told me I needed to focus on the benefits of quitting, and to inscribe the list on paper. To visualize the steps to recovery.

So there it was. Therein lay my difficulty. I did really want to stop, and I had done the list exercise. Repeatedly. I was sick of it. The only steps I could visualize were the steps to the store to buy a pack of cigarettes.

Please don't ever tell addicts they must want to stop. They do.

Please don't tell them to outline all the benefits. They already know them.

On previous occasions when I had quit smoking, I fiercely felt I was making a sacrifice;

I was giving up something. It was always a hell-ish experience. I would look at the infernal benefits list, but sooner rather than later, I acquiesced to the cravings.

༄

Hypnosis—✓
E-cigarette—✓
Cold turkey—✓
Internet help—✓
Self-help books—✓
Cigarettes in jar—✓
Gradual withdrawal—✓
Bets with loved ones—✓
Support system method—✓
Seminars and workshops—✓
Biofeedback tapes and CDs—✓
Quitting for several months—✓
Smoke-in-the-mirror method—✓
Nicotine-replacement therapy—✓
Praying to take addiction away—✓

The above methods have helped many people quit smoking successfully, but not me. I list them to convey how much I desired to quit, but at the same time I became disillusioned that a favorable outcome would come to pass. On one level I genuinely thought each of the above ways would be my miracle cure, especially the one about praying.

Yet deep down inside I didn't seriously think I could quit. I'd heard scores of stories from former smokers who talked about how they still had cravings decades later. I read that smoking alters the hardwiring of the brain. Just what success did I really think I could finally, once and for all, accomplish!

Somehow I would gloss over the *fact* that millions of smokers had quit and never again thought about smoking a cigarette. My confidence I could be victorious had been eroded by the addiction, so that fact meant nothing to me. I believed that for whatever reason, I was a permanent smoker resistant to treatment.

I insisted it was my own personal inescapability to always be addicted. That was it—accept it and move on. Fait accompli.

❦

The thought of my life without a cigarette was beyond my imagination. I lived in agony whenever I tried to quit smoking.

Then one day I stopped. No one was more amazed than me. It still seems incredible.

Getting to that point took forty-four years plus one moment. When the moment hit, it hit me hard. There would be no turning back, and I shall, God willing, forevermore be a nonsmoker.

So from that standpoint, it is easy to quit smoking. It sincerely is.

Withdrawal is also not the difficult part; it's not fun, and it's not something I ever desire to do again. Even so, it is doable.

The hard part is the turn. For those who show a resistance to addiction treatment, making this turn feels impossible and insurmountable. That was how it was for me.

⌀

For years I had desired to be in a romantic relationship, but I'd also felt overwhelmed at the thought of one. A warning pulsated through me that couples lived together with controlling and unkind behavior. I wanted none of that. Even so I am human; I desired intimacy. This issue formed a tug-of-war that played itself out in my involvements.

The dynamic—both of wanting a relationship and also being fearful of one—was not good for me. I kept screaming to get off the emotional roller coaster entanglements I found myself in.

I would only allow myself to enter relationships that had a built-in factor of physical or emotional distance. They were purposely designed to keep me from fully making a commitment to ensure my safety so I wouldn't be hurt. This condition led to tragic irony.

As Fate would have it, I was eventually sent an escalated conflict in the form of a love interest that would catapult me out of this predicament. Usually I felt fairly strong-willed, but right from the start something was amiss. Addictions—this one being a love addiction—do not discriminate.

It was as if this conflict had moved into my psyche, taken over, and set up camp. I became so blinded by what I took for love that, in turn, my safety boundaries were thereby thrown in jeopardy, and consequently I was internally and externally vulnerable to violations.

I tried reasoning and understanding, but the commitment conflict was not going to abdicate control. Slowly I retreated into my supposedly safe world. I suspected this wasn't healthy.

The addiction had won. It had finally isolated me, and had me all to itself.

∽◦

As the years wore on, and oh they did, I grew terribly weary. I spent thousands and thousands of dollars on therapy and traveled thousands and thousands of miles in a search for my self. And to get as far away as possible from the conflict. I had hoped for distance to be that great healer.

Even living where I had fled, around the world in Israel, the addiction was still active. There was nowhere for me to take flight. Upon my return to Texas, I wanted everything ended.

Any real or imagined connection I had associated with the love addiction had placed my life in peril. The pain had become excruciating, and my resolution became how to escape it. I was distraught, and felt in danger.

I must disclose this situation so that you are made aware of the acute and anxious state I had arrived at with this addiction. Otherwise there would have been no turn, no turn at all.

It was this turn that started all the other steps rolling. It brought me to a place to record this to you, and maybe you will find your way to recovery by some spark or step from *Love :: In Code.*

This is my hope. This is my prayer.

I was never going to stop smoking by just giving it up. That ship had sailed for me.

Some people simply stop smoking, or their number comes up after a certain number of attempts. I wasn't in either group. I would have smoked until the day I died.

The love addiction was no different from the smoking addiction. Once I realized I was desperate to extricate myself from the love addiction, that wasn't going to happen.

I was livid no therapist had been able to help me. And I was livid I had not been able to help myself.

In an absolutely hopeless moment when, I cannot stress enough, I felt a critical threat from this love addiction, I also felt there was no one to help me. I had reached a *heightened* sense of urgency, and felt very alone.

In a way I didn't completely understand, because I thought I was close to God, I turned to the Creator. This was the turn.

Step 2

The Prayer

Hope heartens Love.

From my childhood, I felt connected to God. I was drawn to the Judaean Hills in the background of the Bible stories I colored. Recollections are that music and prayer were already intertwined for me; I loved to sing in the children's choir.

Later in life I would make the momentous decision to move and immigrate to Israel. This act of immigration is referred to in Hebrew as *Aliyah*—that means "ascent." I climbed the hilly, cobblestone streets of Jerusalem with the Creator in my heart.

Feeling close, however, is different from turning. To relate this to the physical world, it's as though you're sitting beside someone you're in love with and talking to him, but looking straight ahead. When you turn facing him, and take his hands in yours, the energy changes.

I believe while addictions may assault the physical, mental, emotional, or sexual parts of a person, they are spiritual wounds. Addictions, at their root, are invisible spiritual injuries.

Before the turn I had become increasingly frustrated with my therapy sessions, because I felt I was not getting any better. I had also reached out to a rabbi who, though concerned and considerate, was not able to provide assistance.

In fairness, the therapist who treats by means of psychology or a member of clergy who counsels by virtue of religion could only take me so far. These individuals may be a needed and trusted resource for psychological or religious matters, but they are part of this world, this physical and finite world.

As addictions are ultimately spiritual injuries, at some point they must be eventually treated spiritually. Thus, in this last portion of the journey, I had to go it on my own.

It was upon my physical return to Texas yet still spiritually in Israel, where I was in an unique place to turn and connect to God. I pleaded my case: "Lord, I urgently need your help."

The initial assistance came right away. I was directed toward the study of Kabbalah.

Previously I had taken a few Kabbalah classes before I left for Israel, although while I was there I only studied Hebrew. Now, back in the United States, my Kabbalah studies were more focused.

I was taught how to pray in a way I hadn't known about nor even knew existed. Instead of asking God in my prayers for what I wanted in my life, I began to beseech God for the wisdom to see what God desired of me.

This is a pivotal distinction in the process to a sincere prayer from the heart that I would come to understand by study. We are to be thankful for such enlightment.

Kabbalists describe that essentially the only free will we have is our *intention*. And this is an action of utmost responsibility.

Our intention needs to be directed toward bestowal and goodness rather than the request for our own desires. In constrast to being pre-occupied by what has befallen us, we listen to what God is telling us.

This new method of prayer created an internal seismic shift that began to send spiritual waves all over me, and tuned me into the *intention frequency*. It is in this frequency that we choose the direction of our intention either to love others or selfishly ourselves.

This choice is not as easy to perceive as it may appear, and can be highly deceptive. If we are indeed full of love and charity, is this so we will derive some benefit from this action of goodwill?

Perhaps others will think we are wonderful, and we will be attractive, elevated and needed in their eyes. What is our true intention!

I was not petitioning God to improve my life. I was pleading to save it.

Then I was an addict, and I had reached a risky state I was camouflaging. That's what addicts do, regardless of the addiction.

I knew my options were limited. With what little might I had, I both called out and answered God's call at the exact time.

This occurs in our physical world, too, and can be compared to when we reach for the phone to call someone and they are also calling us. Except in the spiritual world God is constantly calling out to us, but we are trying to hear the ring with our physical ears.

My call was answered immediately and forwarded to Kabbalah and their prayer department! Here I was instructed how to pray.

In that dedicated environment, I would begin to see the *Light* that heals. By that point, the love and smoking addictions had been ongoing for many years.

In a little over a year both my addictions would be gone. Long gone.

❧

Step 3

Love Thyself

Wherever your heart goes, love is sure to Follow.

This new path of prayer presented questions to which I had few answers; I began to investigate. All day and deep into the night I read and researched Kabbalah. I studied and slept with my Tanakh, the Hebrew Bible, beside me. I began to lose track of time. Completely out of character, I even began to lose sight of the days, as well.

I live on the edge of the Texas Hill Country at the end of a Lake Austin inlet. It's living the best of both worlds, i.e. both physical worlds: I'm secluded in the hills but not far from town.

One afternoon I stood up from my desk to stretch from my study and went over to the window to look out beyond to the light through the trees as they swayed in the breeze. My head turned to watch the overflowing creek, full from a recent storm, rush downstream. One by one, a family of deer walked past on the stone pathway. A cat was curled up on a bench soaking up the sun, and a dog sprinted up the steps. A pair of squirrels played hide-and-seek, and a bluebird came to rest upon a nearby branch.

I gasped at this snapshot of Paradise unfolding before my spellbound eyes. A chill swept through me, and an immediate stillness overpowered me. I trembled, and began to cry.

It was there in that moment and in the moments to follow, that for the first time in my life, I began to truly love my spiritual self. I beheld in my heart, and in my soul, and in my hands that I was part of God's spiritual continuum.

The world glistened as if refreshed from a spring rainfall, except there had been none; the rainbow was in my heart. Everyone and everything appeared as though they were wrapped in a translucent special-effects filter. Even driving around familiar streets, my perception had been altered. I had no idea of this at the time, but Kabbalists refer to this spiritual ascension as being *influenced* by the surrounding light as a result of reading Kabbalah texts.

It was as if I had been swimming underwater, unable to hear the people up above by the pool. They'd been eating, drinking, and having a party! I had known they were there, but I couldn't hear them because I was underwater. Then, one day, I surfaced.

I had never authentically loved myself. And now I would. Now I could.

⟳

Kabbalah states we are all in it only for what is in it for ourselves. This is ego. Don't even try to change that principle. *We can't; it's a waste of time.* What we can do is change what we do with that principle.

Even before I was able to love myself, my ego was most certainly still intact. That's what had been throwing me off. I was able to continue through life with the outward appearance I did indeed love myself. Some might even maintain I excelled at that outward appearance!

Within, though, I was not loving, definitely not. I didn't possess spiritual self—love, value, or worth. I was locked behind a door in the house of my soul, and my ego was in charge outside, running the show.

This is a key revelation: if I didn't feel spiritual self-love, I also felt on some level, I wasn't valuable enough to love. Then on some level I felt I wasn't worthy of God's love. Or that God had forgotten about me.

This was not true—God had not neglected me. This was a spiritual injury.

It is in our innermost essence—in our soul—when we feel disconnected from our Creator that our spiritual injuries may manifest in a myriad of mental and emotional disorders. Directly or indirectly, our anger, addictions, anxieties, dissociations, depressions, obsessions, and compulsions may result from our spiritual suffering.

Often we are even unaware we have this sense of separation, because this sensation is of the spiritual world. *It is not a feeling.* So, it is impossible to totally translate this spiritual level in any language, be it English or Hebrew.

The closest description for this sense is the word *peace*, and in Hebrew the word for "peace" is *shalom.* This word also encompasses the definitions of "hello, goodbye, and wholeness." It's not easy to be loving to ourselves, our loved ones, or in our relationship with the Creator when we are in a separated state. If allowed, an active addiction will take precedence over anyone or anything.

As we begin to heal our spiritual self, this sparks a reciprocal action with our emotional self, and we begin to have moments of calm, even, I daresay, a sense of tranquility. Grace, filled with the immense gift of love, goes forth to its intended providence.

Step 4

Love Thy Friend

Love is your heart's Reflection.

Through the prism of our ego, our self-respect is contingent on this finite and financial world. Self-esteem is regulated by the identifiable value of our emotional, intellectual, physical and sexual identity. In this realm, all we do is compare and compete against one another.

It is impossible to truthfully love our friend, someone with whom we aspire to have a soul to soul connection with, when we are in this mode. We may feel less, in some regard, than our friend. Subsequently we spend time and money trying to overcome our covert envy to shore up our shortcomings.

Most of us behave this way unless we have a spiritual plan. Even then, it's a continual challenge!

We do not do anything if it is not directly or indirectly in our self-interest. Our ego provides the motivation to seek out what will benefit us.

Even so, our ego is a vital part of the code, because without recognizing it we would not have the *context* to intuit goodness. Just as in this physical world we wouldn't know that a brisk, sunny day was beautiful if we didn't have a damp, dreary day to provide the opposite force of what constitutes a glorious day.

All roads do lead to righteousness if we stay on the true, existing route. Just as a rainy day can bring nourishment and enchantment. Or a perfect storm. Thus, the good and the bad have the potential to being both good.

Kabbalah does not tell us to get rid of our ego. Quite the contrary. It teaches us to *elevate* it to use for bestowal. Without this expanded ego of selfishness, we would not have the context to know our soul's desire that yearns for selflessness.

Spiritual self-love is not conditional upon the possession of monetary wealth. It is not subject to our age, intelligence, race, religion, or sex. Or attractiveness and accomplishments.

In this world, the message is that our primary worth is our net-worth; we focus on what will financially profit us. Absolutely we need money to live and to provide for our home and family. We work for a sense of security. Yet it is joy that gives rise to happiness.

Here's an illustration: it's a pretty day, and I want to take a walk in the woods. As I traverse down the trail, I look out and my heart opens at the splendor surrounding me. Perhaps a loved one is with me, and we share in this moment together. That is happiness, the emotion of joy. It has nothing to do with money. I may live in the country, and each morning a new dawn greets me on my barefoot stroll.

On the other hand, if I didn't live in the vicinity of a park or nature preserve, then I would need to travel to take my walk. Also, it will be safer to wear shoes or boots for this hike. I'll get hungry, so I want to pack a box lunch, preferably with my favorite gourmet foods. Hey, just because I'm in the woods doesn't mean I don't deserve to eat well. A stylish hat would be nice to take along, too. All that takes money.

Alas, the dollar amount of what we determine our security to be has risen exponentially alongside our expanded egos. We want more things. The commune with nature itself became secondary.

Our financial face value has a higher priority than how we value generosity. This affects our friendships. We become disheartened when we fail to be loving through our emotions. It takes a toll on us.

All too often we allow these emotions to run rampant in our valuable relationships till we have severely damaged them. Or lost them.

When we begin to spiritually love others, goodness follows. *Love thy friend as thyself.*

As our attention turns to others, this creates spiritual vibrations that will reverberate back to us. Yet our intention must be to give fully of our heart to our friend, and not as a means to an end so that we will receive these feel-good effects, or any recognition whatsoever for our effort.

How is this even possible to do since Kabbalah has already stated we are set up in default mode to be self-centered, to only want what is for our own benefit? We've all heard the phrase "The path to hell is paved with good intentions."

There is no question this is an extremely difficult endeavor. It is in our very nature that we are powered up to seek after our own pleasures.

As soon as we reach the desired goal, the gratification dissipates, and we are off looking for either a new thrill, or a new hit of the same one, such as in sports, shopping, and sexual pleasures. Another chase ensues, i.e., we are usually not happy for very long.

The only way to circumvent this spiral is by the compelling awareness and acknowledgment that it is the Creator of All—in control. With this recognition, we are then able to see that heavenly help has stepped in to assist us.

This spiritual transcendence is not a one-time occurence. Each correction of our ego ascends us to the next level closer to the Creator.

It is in this elevated nearness we so desperately desire where our spiritual giving begins to resemble the Creator's own desire to give. It is here, in the image of the Creator where we were created, that we receive eternal pleasure.

The ultimate gift that keeps on giving is when we receive only to give.

Psychology treats the ego, religion avows it, and both submit it for spirituality to direct its course. Transcend it.

Of course, boundaries can be set and honored in this physical world with those individuals who may wish to do us harm. Our success will be determined, in part, by our environment. Although, what is of greater importance is where our spiritual heart of compassion resides, rather than our physical one. In Kabbalah, loving kindness combined with restraint is the emanation of beauty-Tiferet, and beauty and peace are inseparable.

It is when we truly love ourself that we are able to love others, and to feel their love for us. This love asks for nothing, absolutely nothing in return.

True love for others—be it your friend, child, parent, sibling, or spouse—is a spiritual love connection that has no expectations for any emotional or monetary payoff. Your only desire is to fulfill the spiritual desire of the other which is only to have a spiritual connection with you!

Also, romantic love is not what the prevailing view embraces as love. The person we declare "we have fallen in love with" is likely someone who will in someway, somehow or somewhere provide an advantage to us. Our ego typically picks our partners. Then when truth and temptation arrive on schedule, the benefits stop or don't pan out as planned. Love and loyalty begin to vacillate.

God directs us from behind the set to follow goodness, but we choose to rewrite our own screenplay. Our here and now is the pursuit of happiness, so we're going to make a big scene if the script isn't about us.

Now, it would be utterly delightful to report to you that after I made the turn, prayed, and focused on love of myself and others, all was good and well in the world. That a lovefest had arisen from the smoke of my nicotine addiction and the ashes of my love addiction, and I was dancing among the lilies, tambourine in hand, addiction-free.

No. Not quite yet. Both addictions were still up and very much running.

Step 5

Addiction in Action

A concealed heart unlocks to reveal Love.

It was as though a light turned on inside me. A year had passed since I had started to love myself. I was still smoking, but transformation surrounded me. I would smile to myself during my daily comings and goings because it was as if angels were now accompanying me, whispering, "It won't be long now, help is on the way."

An enormous emotional weight had been lifted from me. I was relieved of the symptoms associated with the feeling of low self-worth. Even though nicotine was still a part of my life, I could feel a loosening of its grip on me. Suddenly flush with feeling really, really good for the first time in my life, I didn't care I was having a few cigarettes.

As far as I was concerned with back then (as now), the greater of my two addictions was the love addiction because it was insidious. Yet it would be this very addiction to be the catalyst to my healing.

Then a completely unplanned and unforeseen event arrived. It was as if a camera aperture clicked open in my heart. Click. Then, rather quickly as it had opened, it closed. Click.

In that compressed time span during which the aperture was fully extended, a flash of light entered my heart as though a spiritual surgeon had opened me up to do exploratory surgery. With this exposure, I could see up-close the addiction in action.

Until that moment—and this is so important—I *knew* I had addictions. I just could not see them. Despite the fact I surely saw my hand reach to my mouth with each and every puff, I could not see the addiction itself.

The second I saw this, I was stunned, totally speechless. I couldn't believe what I observed. I had been going on about my life all the while the addictions were operating right in front of me!

I could acutely feel for the first time the love addiction's obsessive grasp on me. I was able to see with complete clarity that the cigarette I reached for during the day was nothing more nor less than a nicotine addiction.

In rapid succession—this was all happening in a matter of moments—I saw that I was an addict and that addicts hurt themselves. And I didn't want to hurt myself, because I now loved myself. I didn't want to be an addict.

So I stopped. Not immediately, but I did stop. That was it.

I purposely didn't stop either addiction at once. The reasons were twofold. First, I was in some sort of state of *shock* coming into this awareness, and second, I didn't want my quitting to be an *impulsive* reaction. I wanted the cessation of both to come from truth.

I promptly set a combined quit date for a few weeks later. When that day came, I stopped. Both.

Step 6

Self-Care — Protection

Love is a force of Purity.

Everywhere speakable and unspeakable traumas exist. It is difficult to have faith and forgive, much less love, when we have been placed in harm's way.

When we feel we are not valued, we may deem we are not worthy to be loved. We may question God's care for us. Why would a benevolent Creator allow any affliction, an impure force, to even happen? A separation from God occurs and this devises a level of concealment from the Creator.

God's frequency range starts to fade-in and fade-out. Our questioning of God's care for us amplifies into questioning of the actual Creator.

Thus, our natural, encoded ability to love becomes, in part, impaired. Spiritually compromised, our wall of emotional self-protection is weakened. Our conduct is usually out of control in some way, but we're definitely out of code.

Addictions discern any opportunity to move in and take over, and they do. Quickly.

It's not just addictions that strategize this maneuver, either. Anger and anxiety beat a path to this unlatched door, too.

This separation caused my instinctual reaction for self-preservation to be suspended to the degree that it permitted the gatekeeper to grant access to the addictions. I was hooked.

As I *spiritually* self-loved, this healed my *emotional* self that signaled for the reestablishment of greater *physical* self-protection boundaries. *There was a renewal of body, and a resilience of spirit.*

My soul began to respond as I began to authentically self-love from a place of truth and not from a place of ego fulfillment. My system restored to code. Over time a level was reached where my emotional and physical body began to naturally and instinctually want to reject the addictions.

One way of achieving this was through the ability to see the addiction in action via the harmful addictive element—the nicotine for the smoking addiction and the control for the love addiction. When my self-safekeeping returned, a level of concealment was lifted where I could finally witness these destructive elements.

As you spiritually self-love, an addiction's power over you becomes disabled. Then it will not be a struggle to go into recovery, and put yourself through withdrawal; it will be a struggle not to.

When I look back and review some of the self-help books I had read, I can see the actual words *self-protection* on the page. I was not in a place to emotionally comprehend the passage.

If I didn't feel self-love, why on earth would I want to self-care? The self-protection had to come through the love. It was a progression of the code.

It would have remained impossible for me to achieve a *sustainable* recovery from my addictions had I continued to live a life by where my self-esteem was dependent—a form of addicted—upon my ego, and I had not ascended to a *spiritual* self-love level. Also, I would have been and still be exposed to a higher rate of relapse.

∽◎

A special note to you, dear *Love :: In Code* readers:

Please stop for a moment, wherever you are, and simply look around you. You may be alone or surrounded by others. Think about your life.

Addictions put you at risk in every possible way. They will control your emotional and physical health, and will seek to ruin you financially.

A spiritual presence is with you—at every step, yet it is almost impossible to see this presence when pain has taken over your faith. Your very essence is precious, and your intrinsic worth is a valuable part to the world.

Perhaps, at present, it barely seems perceptible for you to feel good, much less precious, but this is the truth. When you see a glimmer of light, and you will, go for it.

∽◎

Each person has their own withdrawal symptoms with their own addiction. If there is more than one attempt at quitting, each time may vary in symptoms.

Of my two addictions, one was physically damaging, and one was emotionally harmful. Recovery from each took a similar path.

My previous attempts at quitting smoking weren't pretty; I needed the fix. When I had tried quitting smoking before, the cravings loomed large in my mind and I succumbed to the anxiety. It was beyond any thought I could ever be a nonsmoker, and for that reason I always relapsed.

This time as I approached my final quit date, it was as if my mental state had become organizer extraordinaire. It informed the withdrawal system I was going to be sick for a while and needed to be healed. It further decreed to the addiction it would be going away. And by the way, no need to ever return because it would not be welcome anymore. That is exactly what happened.

Here is my personal list of withdrawal symptoms during the first days of my nicotine recovery: lightheadedness, coughing, tightness in my lungs, headache, fatigue and insomnia together.

I didn't drive the first two days, because as my oxygen levels adjusted to normal I felt lightheaded enough to warrant that decision. The most intense symptoms peaked about day three, but I did experience all of them to some level, though gradually tapering off, for several months.

As the nicotine physically withdrew from my body this concluding time, I didn't undergo any panic associated with needing a cigarette. I did feel nicotine-related twinges, and a craving for sweets as my system recalibrated, and I would drink water to flush my system out.

I've *never once* had any euphoric recall of wanting a cigarette. Now the desire to smoke a cigarette is akin to my desire to chase after harm—it doesn't exist. I had stopped on occasion before, but this time I have no thought whatsoever to smoke.

With the love addiction, once I was in possession of spiritual self-love, it was as if a switch was thrown. The actual obsession was over.

The *passion* of the very love and my *persistence* to disengage from the dependency created my awakening. Simply, on an emotional level, the control I felt my past relationships had over me was the equivalent of the constraint I had over my own feelings. Profoundly, on a spiritual level, it was the Creator's desire to draw me closer.

A romantic relationship will be a blessing filled with kindness and goodness. It will be a soulful connection where the Divine Essence dwells in our midst. An everlasting pleasure of sexual coupling will emerge with the presence of spiritual coupling.

The addictions were healed in my spiritual transcendence, and the correspondence that I felt in this physical world was freedom. Laughter, which has been an important part of my life, became more spontaneous.

With each day all my withdrawal symptoms lessened, and I felt a little stronger in my addiction recovery. Over time, they quietly diminished. One day I awoke, and they were no longer there.

Step 7

Spiritual Recovery—Peace

And the meager shall inherit the land,
and delight themselves in an abundant peace.
Psalm 37:11

In Hebrew, the word "land" is *eretz* and associated with the name for "desire" *ratzon*. Spiritually I interpret this lovely verse as it is those who seek altruism over egoism will receive their soul's truest desire, and shall delight in a greater well-being. Peace will only reign in this world with one heart—Oneness.

Even on days that are distressing, as this is life, I now have a feeling of joyful belonging. Each new addiction-free day is never taken for granted, and I will feel thankful for ever and ever for my recovery.

At the close of every sixth day commences *Shabbat* — a sabbath "to cease to exist, to be ended." In this space a bridge is extended for us between this physical, finite earth to the spiritual, eternal Heaven. To attain this elevation will require effort, but the reward will be extensive.

Filled with magnificence, the seventh day was declared holy. This world becomes incandescent when we turn our eyes to behold all that is wondrous.

Quintessencially, we are all created as explorers of the soul. Whether our quest is to travel the high seas or follow a quiet road leading from our doorstep, it is the radiance of our enduring love that will illuminate our path's return to each other.

So I do hope with all my heart, dear *Love :: In Code* readers, that you have been able to perceive that the very pleasure we seek is the spiritual world. And it is not faraway.

It is here, and surrounds us. It is love.

The Creator has sent us every state,
and every moment out of love to unite with us,
so that we, in turn, will experience
never-ending Love.
This is the Code.
This is Love :: In Code.

Barbara Permilla Roth

The Song of Songs
Verse 6:3
I am my Beloved's and my Beloved is mine.

אֲנִי לְדוֹדִי וְדוֹדִי לִי